Gravity Assist

Martha Silano

Distributed by Independent Publishers Group
Chicago

Gravity Assist

Martha Silano

Distributed by Independent Publishers Group
Chicago

Saturnalia Books
105 Woodside Rd.
Ardmore, PA 19003
info@saturnaliabooks.com

ISBN: 978-1-947817-00-5
Library of Congress Control Number: 2018910480

Book Design by Robin Vuchnich
Printing by Versa Press
Cover Art: Robin Vuchnich

Author Photo: Langdon Cook

Distributed by:
Independent Publishing Group
814 N. Franklin St.
Chicago, IL 60610
800-888-4741

Poems from this book were originally published in the following journals:

32 Poems: "I am the miraculous" and "My Environs"
Adroit Poetry Journal: "X"
The Awl: "Tributary"
AGNI: "Adjacent to the Way"
American Poetry Journal: "The Mechanical Hope Contraption" and "It will have started as a small comb"
The Cincinnati Review: "The World" and "When I saw the loblolly pine,"
CityArts: "Time for art in the cosmos is very short,"
Copper Nickel: "Still Life with Motorcycle Revving, Wailing Siren, American Goldfinch Trill"
Crab Orchard Review: "This highway's a ribbon,"
DIAGRAM: "Report Your Unusual Phenomenon"
Fogged Clarity: "The Chamber of Silence"
The Fourth River: "The New Nature Poem"
Glass: A Journal of Poetry: "Yes, of course"
Heron Tree: "On a Job Listing for a Copepod Collector"
Kestrel: "Because the Dead Never Vanish"
Konundrum Engine Literary Review: "Dear Mr. Wordsworth,"
The Inquisitive Eater: "Ode to a Bell Pepper"
The Monarch Review: "Space Probe Pantoum"
New Ohio Review: "My Mother Who Told Me"

North American Review: "Gift Tower"
Notre Dame Review: "Nearly Every Songbird on Earth Is Eating Plastic"
Orion: "Peach Glosa"
Pithead Chapel: "Lately my gratitude's"
Pittsburgh Poetry Review: "Jealous"
Poetry: "Song of Weights and Measurements" and "Ode to Autocorrect"
Prairie Schooner: "1961"
Redheaded Stepchild: "Dear Absolute Certainty,"
Sequestrum: "Verge" and "Questions for Your Shadow"
South Dakota Review: "Scorching Sinkhole Renga"
Southern Humanities Review: "The Trilobites"
Southern Indiana Review: "Gerbils in Space" and "Break-Away Effect"
Sou'wester: "Beneath twelve feet of ashy topsoil,"
Superstition Review: "Despite Nagging Malfunctions"
Tahoma Literary Review: "No, it did not give you wings,"
Thrush: "Bumblebees Are Made of Ash"
Watershed Review: "Tornado"
Waxwing: "Instead of a father"
Water-Stone Review: "Hummingbirds of the World"

"Here I am," appears in *The Crafty Poet, A Portable Workshop*, edited by Diane Lockward (Wind Publications, 2013).

"The World" won *The Cincinnati Review*'s 2013 Robert and Adele Schiff Poetry Award.

"Gerbils in Space" was featured on *Verse Daily*, November 24, 2014.

"Dear Absolute Certainty," is reprinted in *The Crafty Poet 2, A Portable Workshop*, Ed. Diane Lockward (Terrapin Books, 2016).

The editors at *Southern Humanities Review* nominated "The Trilobites" for a 2017 Pushcart Prize.

Immense appreciation and thanks to Washington State Artist Trust, Centrum Writers Foundation, The Helen Riaboff Whiteley Center, Artsmith, Camac Centre D'Art, and The Corporation of Yaddo for providing time and the space to work.

For their inspiration, writing prompts, encouragement, keen editorial eyes and, most of all, their friendship, I am deeply thankful to Kelli Russell Agodon, Molly Tenenbaum, Susan Blackwell Ramsey, Diane Seuss, Erin Malone, Megan Snyder-Camp, Kathleen Flenniken, Laura Shoemaker, Moira Linehan, Tina Kelley, Sara Stockton, and Joelle Bielle.

For his genius and geniality, I remain incomparably indebted to Rex Gentry, MD.

This book is for Lang, Riley, and Ruby.

Table of Contents

II. Orbit Insertion

III. Escape Velocity

Song of Weights and Measurements

For there is a dram.
For there is a farthing.
A bushel for your thoughts.
A hand for your withered heights.

For I have jouled along attempting
to quire and wisp.

For I have sized up a mountain's meters,
come down jiffy by shake to the tune
of leagues and stones.

For once I was your peck-ish darling.

For once there was the measure
of what an ox could plow
in a single morning.

For once the fother, the reed, the palm.

For one megalithic year I fixed my gaze
on the smiling meniscus, against the gray wall
of graduated cylinder.

For once I measured ten out of ten
on the scale of pain.

For I knew that soon I'd kiss goodbye
the bovate, the hide and hundredweight.

For in a each pinch of salt, a whisper of doubt,
for in each medieval moment, emotion,

like an unruly cough syrup bottle, uncapped.
For though I dutifully swallowed

my banana doses, ascended, from WELCOME
to lanthorn, three barleycorns at a time,

I could not topple the trudging, trenchant cart.

For now I am forty rods from your chain and bolt.
For now I am my six-sacked self.

I. Periapsis

Here I am,

weed-whacking with a spatula
flipping hash browns with an emory board
filing my nails with a knife

Suddenly I know precisely
what to do with these tears
though already they're smoldering

Here I am
hedge clipping
the wine-stained flutes

shard-scatter like a flock
of merlin-shocked sanderlings
With a needle I'm digging up

the something stupid I said
to the sand crabs
to the rising tide

Here I am
with the spoke before I thought
with the sizzling sea

with this most unhelpful implement

Despite Nagging Malfunctions

I was born with a stainless-steel spoon, licked it
through bloomer-less somersaults, asbestos tiles
unleashing from cafeteria ceilings, through lectures
teeming with chalky arrows of inscrutable vectors.
To revive me I was given *Halicephalobus mephisto*,
nematode residing in the sulfurous dark of the TauTona
gold mine, *mephisto* in honor of Mephistopheles,
he who loves not the light. In lieu of high honors
I sniffed the sweat of the men who assembled
the Voyager space probes, pungency of metal melting.
I was given, most graciously, Tycho Brahe's
prosthetic copper nose and tinged-green skull,
his unfixing of the forever fixed stars (*Oh thick wits.*
Oh blind watchers of the sky.). I fell in love
with Fornax, Latin for *furnace*, divine impersonation
of oven, Roman Goddess of baking bread, constellation
from which we gander at galaxy UDFj-39546284,
most distant object in the universe. Mother: *The world*
is so much better when you're upside down.
Father: manic physicist. One morning, Kepler
turned a photometric eye on Cygnus-Lyra, commenced
its pursuit of sun-roasted orbs for the habitable.

Advice to myself: don't be sure every wink
is a warm body, a covey of benthic tubeworms
nestled around a hydrogen-sulfide-spewing
black-smoker hearth. Advice to you? I have
none—only this spoon I invite you to sip from,
these nematodes at home in 160-degree steam,
grazing on bacteria that would kill us.

It will have started as a small comb

in the eaves of the house

       with a basement where you kept your lab mice

in the eaves of the house

       where the moths hid beneath the leathery laurel

in the living room

       between living and dying

between the bedroom and the mirror

       the hallway and the rotary phone

the driveway and the oil stains

       the ivy strangling the oak

the rhododendron that croaked

       which was the moment you decided

forever was worse than dying

       in the house which was the sun-porch

the cold room the stairwell

       the stifling attic the roof

which was the ladder he lugged

       toward the nest of hornets

the ladder no one could steady

       but him

head shrouded

       in a tattered flannel shirt

fumigating the moment

       which was the language

of multiple stings

       lexicon of a stinger lodged

releasing more venom

       when you tried to pull it out

Doomed Moon

Saturn's rings may have been created by an unnamed moon that disappeared 4.5 billion years ago – The Daily Galaxy

An unnamed moon.
                    Baby Bianca, Darling Dione.
Her outer layers wintry.
                    On a morning stroll in her Britax B-Agile,
unwittingly whammed
                    into something larger, something saturnine,
someone in need
                    of her lucent cold,
her frost-bound frigorific.
                    A big thing wants to be bigger;
Saturn signed on as accomplice.
                    Not a moon-on-moon clash
or the rings would be rocky.
                    Doomed moon diving
toward death,
                    bereft of its bluster;
doomed moon unnamed,
                    neither Janus nor Fornjot,
not Hyperion nor Pallene,
                    gelid stripped away on impact,
hydrogen shroud
                    inducing a knack for creating/
destroying. For a thousand decades
                    the spiraling loops
ten to a hundred times larger.
                    Icy spheres birthing
the new—Epimetheus, Tethys.
                    Alterations, actions,
anything but static:
                    all this doomsday drama,
all this shimmery ruination.

My Mother Who Told Me

the Bible's a Mount Everest of metaphor—
the seventh day more likely the eight
trillionth, the Holy Spirit about as real

as Casper the Friendly Ghost. My mother
who never once definitively sang
in the tune of Judgment, the lexicon

of flames. My equivocating, not-sure-he's-
the-Savior mother, who calls with an urgent
message: Billy Graham's 95th birthday special.

Mother of Peace, mother who sanctioned
my Sunday school exodus when the teacher
refused to define adultery, who rolled her eyes

at shiny offering plates, who *yadda yadda'd*
the Lord's Prayer, mother too busy browsing
The Female Eunuch to read aloud from

the book of Jonah, to reason a man could live
three days in the belly of a whale, mother
lacking sufficient conviction to share the story

of the loaves and fishes, inciting me to fall
to my knees as I did one day in 1974,
the man on the screen having told me I must.

1961

It was the year they coined all-you-can-eat,
so when we tucked our paper napkins under our chins

bowls and platters line-danced each time we said
enough already, I'm full! Suddenly we had back-

talk, a word to describe that *but Mahhhhhhhhhh* whine.
And when a girl insisted she had to have Malibu Barbie,

didn't say please, begged for the Peter Max sheets, we
had a word for her now, and it was bratty. Because

a draft warranted dodging, we got draft-dodger,
because a war in the jungle had been smoldering

six interminable years, we got no-win. It was the year
Heinlein busted out grok, an understanding so thorough

and deep, the lonesome soul gave way to the drippy mascara
of the group, and when she did, a malapportioned nitpicker,

a sexy attendee, could write it all down in a memo,
or else zap her sorrows in a microwave while gazing

at moon shots. That was the year of the walk-in,
where a dishy gal didn't need to call ahead for a shampoo

and set, a towering bee-hive. While Ray Charles belted out
"Unchain My Heart," we were Skidooing our skyjacks,

sleeping in, tuning out in the key of Valium, softlanding
our power broker spacecrafts, trying on permissivism.

Back then everyone was a unitarded, wheeling-and-dealing
paparazzo; it was all fab, no trade-offs, round-the-clock zazzy.

Someone said wazoo, so wazoo it was, and we were psyched,
so very psyched, even while servicing our modules, even

when we were trying on our reentry schtick, sidling up,
for the gillionth time, to the buffet line, loading our plates

with splash down.

Instead of a father

a volcano. A girl puzzling through long division between eruptions. A girl working hard to discern the intervals between disturbances. It was a kind of having to duck from the pumice. It was like the chunk of anthracite in your 3rd grade classroom, the one the teacher couldn't stop talking about. It was like the chained dogs at Pompeii—it was that pitch, one of the many greatest hits of the 70s. Steadfast like breathing in the finest particles, the ones that lodge in your blood. Like a cubic mile of ash and mud and rock. A seismic jolt followed by an explosion. It was like a heat surge scorching every eukaryotic cell, its Golgi apparatus, its smooth endoplasmic reticulum and its rough endoplasmic reticulum, each *you kernel* singed.

Bloodline

Any day the floor will give.
By the time he dies the fifty dust-
catching hand-painted wooden roosters
dragged from his sister's Miami condo will
eke out a prayer for her final reclusive night when,
fricasseed on booze, she dropped to the parquet
ground, the arm not hugging the toilet
hugging her final jug of Smirnoff.

In his hide-away office, reams of unsolved problems,
just enough torsion equipment to tax the clay foundation.
Kate, his other sister, same illness: racks and racks of
labels-on frocks, boxes of stylish pumps stacked to the ceiling.
Mom had to clear off the bed before she could tuck us in.

Nope, won't let me throw away a thing. Very attached.
Okay, I say, but can't stop thinking of packing day—
pulleys, trolleys, motion centers, vacuum tubes, clamps.

Quietly, he accumulated a dozen behemoth PCs.
Rheology, from *rheo*: "flow." *Soft bodies pressured to wince.*
Someone's gotta want at least a gross of transistors,
teaching materials on liquid-to-liquid transition.

Urge him to toss just a few of these atoms and bonds?
Very touchy. Wadded up a few ditto sheets, circa 1966—
wow, did he go ape shit. Doesn't want anyone near it.

Except for his diaries – those he's saving for you.
Yah. Maybe you can use them to add a little
zest to your poems. You're the writer: have at it.

Report Your Unusual Phenomenon

Seen it myself as a girl—flare the size of a jet plane.

Raced to tell my mother, who told me not to lie.

And why should a mother, why should anyone,

these will-o'-the-wisps gone wild, this spun silk

spattering brilliant streams, this yellow washtub

bouncing down a boulevard, traveling a city block,

crashing into a barn, killing the horse inside?

Why this buttery *boules de feu*, this *kugelblitz*

riding the center lane, buzzing the Sunday ham,

these sparkly basketballs striking the Golden Temple,

carving trenches, bulldozing peat, busting down doors?

Came at me like a comet. Blew my shirt right off.

Sizzled and crackled like bacon frying,

like candle flames not three feet from my nose.

Several physicists, a loud crash, my sanity,

especially here in the Midwest. Not some sort

of wacko President of Find the Children.

Half the timeframe fuzzy, but it rotated

on the sill like two fists, coiled tinsel,

a traffic signal blinking amber, a novelty

glass ball. Fizzed like one of those fizzer sticks.

I knew no one'd believe me, that feeling

of taking clothes from a dryer, but they weren't

chirping, not at all in a Figure 8, so I hung up

quickly. Just a blue mist, loose screw, ringing phone.

A hammer made of tinfoil, a hula-hoop of light.

Just me and my dear daddy (daddy saw it too).

Just leaving the house the same way it arrived.

Tributary

Either everything's a valley, a jelly donut
dimpled down the middle, or else everything's

a collision of plates, crustal thickening on its way
toward muscled mountains. Either everything's way,

way, beyond mid-gallop or a rundown shack haystack-
still, a dog-patch immobilizing glory, gumption, get up

and go. Either everything's a sandy path leading
to a dune-saving fence or nothing's guarded, out of reach.

Which is worse: too many walls or not enough,
the laciness of shams or an endless hallway of bare

jalousies, a dead fly lounging on each lone pane?
Everything's a spider, filling up on gnats, building/

breaking its web; that is, unless nothing's a spider,
including the spider whose web is a map. Either

everything is happening or it's quieter than a feeder
bereft of its pecking/twirling flicker. Either everyone

is needing something, a jump or a stroke, or else
it's a mojito in the lotus position, cancer punching

its melanomic clock. Neuron for neuron, fly brains
outclass the ones loaded down with *game change,*

watershed-moment, tipping point. Also haven't
figured out how to navigate by stars.

Dear Absolute Certainty,

Here's a domain just for you: *math.com*,
prisms and pyramids, area of a polygon,

the power of x. Like Prince said *I guess*
I shoulda known, only I didn't, or not enough

about classifying angles, congruent figures,
the formula for volume. Thank you, *2piR*,

2a + 2b, for certain beyond unquestionable,
for the stupefying quiz at unit's end.

You call it a root; I'll call it a clothesline.
Together we'll get the dishes done,

and no one will go home empty-place-
holdered. My eclipse, my unknown,

I'm honoring you with a pair of forever
lines, with a cosine I've just replaced

with a conundrum. Dear Pythagoras/
nebulous, this triangle's got three legs—

one's the curlicue of a question mark,
the others dangle like the legs of a wasp.

I should be backing slowly away,
but *I guess I must be dumb* like a frog pond

dusted with pollen. Wanting to thank you,
but instead I'm falling backwards

into a cloud like a giant mutt—though wait,
it's a pair of pterosaurs, a skull.

X

Man, we'll never know what's real. It's just gonna be
a head banger's ball until the end of eternity.
  —MUFON meeting, Portland, Oregon

They saw it from the capsule, thought it might've been
the final stage of a Saturn V, but when they radioed Houston,

learned it was 6,000 nautical miles away, and anyway
their puzzlement shaped like a dumbbell. Or was it a dome,

burst of light and whoosh, more like *daylight but red light—*
planets with Christmas lights on, over California, over Russia,

over San Juan. Large-eyed and molten, as in *this is not a prank*
phone call! I got three of 'em: yellow, green, and blue, a shiny

horizontal silver dollar *but we couldn't, you know, blurt it out.*
Skipping over water, *and they decide what's real,* so recant

or cover up, call it a weather balloon, strike from the record
the words *I saw it,* call it Project Grudge, don a thought-screen

helmet (*only two failures since 1958*). Transparent, acrid
insectoid clinging to his trousers. Or was it belladonna? Departing

spaceship, or a Citroen on the M8 motorway? We have a red-eyed
sperm critter; we are being escorted, dragged to the ground.

Like the lid on the pot of my grandmother's kielbasa—
the never-to-be known, all of it crackling.

Questions for Your Shadow

Who is she?
Do you agree?
Does she come from the pit or the surface epidermis?

Who buried her?
Is she more like an olive or a caper?
Did she burrow unnoticed, or did you miss that creepy-crawly twitch?

Whether or not she swooned: does it matter?
Was she the wasabi pea of faux pas?
Did she travel to places like Tasmania

before the native snakes were gobbled up
by cane toads? When it began to rain,
how did she greet the leeches?

Is she bitter? Is she precise? Toasted or raw?
Was she willing to gift her left ear
to a friend? Is her face a jinx?

Did she track down mud in the Mojave?
Will she get to hell before her father?
When the fight is over will she continue to punch?

Will her wolves be sated while her sheep graze?
Do mushrooms sprout in her mouth?
Does her thief's hat burn?

Was she swiped in the nose for asking,
kicked for being alive?
Did he catch her like a fly in his fist?

Did they spoil her with butter and limes?
How come they could not catch her
like wind in a net?

No, it did not give you wings,

that month in the hospital, believing
you were dead. No lift, no day of feasting.

Father broke your faith, a transitive verb,
Father believed, intransitive (How do you

know? It says so on page 28). Required
to take a father's vantage as Gabriel's Horn,

words of some book you were forced
to read. He + present + certain. He + present

+ qualm. *I'm sure. He's elusive. We doubt.*
Neither/both insist. Jesus did /

did not ascend. (Daddy wasn't sure.)
Couldn't rewrite that sentence as a string

of morphemes; break each phrase
into tense and verb, perhaps, but not

revision—*gone* to *reborn, hem and haw* to *belief,*
take a clipped and grounded thing, make it soar.

Notes on Gravitational Forces

Since the week before I was born, someone figured out Gravity Propelled Space Travel.

Since by dusk you can find me, hose in hand, watering the zucchini my daddy called *googootz*

Since it had been proven mathematically that exploration of most of our solar system would be impossible.

Since there was a need to scribble out, erase, recalculate.

Since the energy change generated by a swing-by sends an object farther and farther into space.

Since he taught me how to locate the Seven Sisters in a hazy sky.

Since I taught him nothing, not even escape.

Since the mass of a smaller object is affected by the pull of two bodies, but those bodies do not feel that object's influence.

Since I am always imagining the blooming forsythia before he hacked it.

Since flybys make it possible to explore the entire solar system, planet by planet, indefinitely.

Since keeping a secret is like keeping a corpse in your pocket.

Since it had been mathematically proven to be impossible.

Since I'd had enough of hating, rose hips without the rose.

Since it had nothing to do with Newton's third law of motion.

Since the smell of what he did, swarm of flying ants after a frost.

Since the high-energy barrier was destroyed.

Since I appear in his dreams, since he appears in mine.

Since one must be willing to fail with accuracy.

Since I think you understand what is and isn't breakable.

The Chamber of Silence,

where quiet does not calm but claims,
a sound-absorbing shell forbidding

the comfort of even a doctor's footsteps
on a shiny linoleum floor. Lighting altered

to lose all sense of time, silence deeper
than any in the Arctic, the Urals.

Cosmonauts, bereft of their Pushkin,
their Ukrainian folksongs, stifling

the urge to cry out, sound of nothing
like icy waves giving way to flames.

Lack of chirping cricket, scurrying mouse,
lonesome wail of a factory whistle, gurgling

and splashing of a rising Volga River.
Siberian silence—two inseparable sisters

no longer speaking. Echo-less room
where books, palette, paintbrush, paper

and pen are forbidden. It might be a day,
days, a week or more (they never say).

Minute by minute, silence morphing
to a deafening let me out! Every ounce

of will to keep one's mind: *Poyekahli!*
("Off we go!"), to rise in a trembling

rocket, gaze on a glittering sickle, one's home
an orb. To, awestruck, orbit, become a cloud

of racing fire, roll three times through waving wheat,
land face first in a field never smelling as sweet.

II. Orbit Insertion

My Environs

I say warbling vireo and

a turbo-jet drops from my tongue.

I say trill while a mower groans away

the cottonwood breeze. A bird says *If I see you,*

I'm gonna seize you and squeeze you till you squirt

as a line of cars slashes its psalm like lenticels

on bark. How best to solve this natural/

unnatural dichotomy if not by clapping one

or both hands? *Scritch*, says the squirrel,

x, x, x, say those who solve for *y,* bye-bye

says the glacial moraine. I am multiplying

existence times the peculiar tufts of dozing

owls. Mice make their own sound. Who

can say who's more astonished? A person

mishears *momentous* as *moment,* falls into

a verdant complacency, sleepy as a dog

on a rug where nothing/everything's in flux.

When I saw the loblolly pine,

its furrowed bark, I knew I was close
to fully understanding when a bird
is gone it's gone, the last one,
the end, done, as my daughter
used to say, like the Carolina Parakeet,
menace removed from having a name
in Seminole: *pot pot chee. Kelinky*
in Chickasaw. Pest that got in the way
of tobacco and cotton, adornment
for a lady's hat, an index card's
worth of grief. Their greatest fault:
returning to the place where one
had been shot, otherwise known
as unfortunate flocking behavior.
From the perspective of the moon,
it looks familiar, doesn't it? Returning
and returning to the small-scale
garden plot where your dead brother
lay, scent of dying like a rotting rowboat
beside the Pascagoula Quik-Mart.
There's no fundraiser big enough
to bring them back, no amount
of money to pledge. Because
they loved corn, tore open
apples to reach the seeds,
because their distress calls
could be heard for miles,
there's a little less wonder
along the Perdido River.

The World

...the unexplainable in nature makes me feel the world is big—far beyond my understanding —Georgia O'Keeffe

The world so big, so big and beyond, tumbleweed so turbulent in the wind, the cormorants of the world so sunning themselves on shit-stained piers.

World a big son with his big boy accretion, his magnesium need for the screen, his Xbox lithosphere. The world and the calderas

of the world and the peaks of the world with their toothsome fissures toppling the calm. The world with its spiral notebook of incomprehensible:

$$R = \frac{v2 \sin 20}{g}$$

beside a bleached and broken skull, conundrum drum imbued with the screwy. Molten, turgid world, sodden and still,

still world trombone-huge beside the porcine circovirus that is its belly's molten dark, its pretty-please misery, its unborrowed sorrow. World

so big and silent, with equatorial bulge, cannot speak but hails from a bigger that blew apart, knocks upon our rutabaga dumbness.

Big boy with big boy tilt, his Chandler Wobble, would smother the family cat with pumice kisses; this big-bang progeny making of a seafloor

a butter-and-eggs and blazing star prairie, for he is the feline of reinvention, of meander. Oh, the lengths we will go to de-shellac, deglaze, to root out

the wingless and withered, that whirring noise either nothing or something in this world, with its *dis-n-that* roar, its difficult marriage of yellow jacket

and woodpile. World swelling like the rising Seine, with resolve, with eddies
and revolutions, with ranting, red-dressed volcanoes, world buxom enough

for eighteen classes of nouns, each distinguished by its own unique suffix.
Curl in the tip of a tail, come-hither unretractable tongue, voluptuous world

woozy with the blue beyond the pelvic bone's socket: frosty, flanged, fecund.

Gerbils in Space

And geckos. Fruit flies, kernels of corn.
Amoebas and bacteria. Black mice

and white mice. Once upon a time a dog
named Laika ascended in Sputnik 2,

egregious PR on account of no plan
for a safe return. But once they figured out

re-entry, up went Belka and Strelka,
public support. Two Russian tortoises,

a posse of mealworms, a few dozen
wine flies, all aboard Zond 5, first

orbiting of the moon. Before a human
could venture into weightlessness,

six rhesus monkeys named Albert preceded,
each one charmed with his own uniquely

abysmal end—explosions, suffocation,
failing parachutes. The French launched

Felicette, electrodes jammed beneath
feline skin, transmitting her condition

to the safely on the ground. More than hers,
a hundred miles above our penny-loafered feet,

I wonder about the condition of the brains
beneath bouffanted, mop-topped heads,

of a wavering between staunchest enemies
and let's-do-this-moon-thing-together friends.

A dozen gerbils 350 miles above me as I type,
high-tech gadgets sucking up ethereal waste

for the broken-free and the gravity-blessed—
for the constantly pulled in, constantly falling back.

Dear Mr. Wordsworth,

It turns out there is no tranquility. Signed,
The 21st Century.

However, there is powerful feeling. Other things
are powerful too—

the same old powerful things (waterfalls, strength
of a daffodil stem)—

some of them newly-minted (GBU-39, *for ultra surgical strikes*).
Dear Mr. Wordsworth,

It turns out my son had slippage this June-uary spring,
neglected not only his teeth

but the last four weeks of geography homework,
which means that today,

instead of slipping into a tranquil bath, I'm steeped
in prehistoric Peru;

in recollection's place, I get interruption, swimming
smack into Pedro,

five-foot penguin with a seven-inch beak; instead of my heart
with pleasure filling,

10,000 cobs in the Valley of Tehucan,
the barking dog timer (did I not

mention I was tending flapjacks?). No, Mr. Wordsworth,
no tranquility to be summoned

while I pull from my son's gargantuan backpack the crumpled nest
marked *D*.

Did you, Mr. Wordsworth, get Ds? Do you even know
what D stands for? Nope, not Daffodil!

Mr. Wordsworth: procurement and concealment,
and I'm not talking the inward eye.

His teacher called it slippage. Tranquil's in the gun safe,
nodding jocundly with the jonquils.

Mr. Wordsworth? Consider it downright twinkling you had no power
outages, no power to speak of.

No twice-a-day-right clock, no dead bulb in the dark,
dark dawn.

Pick and Choose: To on-the-couch lay
or neigh like a jackass?

To spontaneously overflow, out-do the sparkling waves,
toss one's head

in a sprightly dance, flutter and crowd and host, or stand
at the sink, sponging the morning's mournful cutlery?

Coots on a Lake

Someone said safety in numbers.
Someone called them prey with wings.
Someone called us prey with hands and feet.
Someone who noticed how tightly they flock
never bothered to learn the name of the bird
in the brambles plaintively whistling *we're fucked.*

On a Job Posting for a Copepod Collector

They were looking for someone to round up a thousand,
and I was their girl. Who else but me, with my degrees in tear-

shaped bodies, in heartlessness? What else would I need
but a bucket, a low-tech fish net, a set of close-up-

and-personal eyes, what else but my reverential respect
for the exoskeleton-ed? My plan: explain my penchant

for leaf litter, hydrothermal vents, my endless pursuit
for all things ephemeral—gone-tomorrow puddles

and ponds, temporarily damp moss, the water-filled recesses
of bromeliads and pitcher plants, intertidal splash pools.

I know it would be a daily drop-to-my-knees situation
attempting to glimpse those four antennae (two long,

two exceedingly small), to witness the miraculous
sussing of predator versus prey via flowing water

analysis; I know as I cozied up with one of Earth's
most burly creatures, my life would become,

like theirs, a lesson in absorption, in transparency, which
is why I'm a shoe-in, especially when I tell them

it's a job like any other—repairing cracked water mains,
sweeping popcorn from the aisles— requiring focus

on the fact of a single eye, the realization we're all bio-
indicators, exposing the havoc our tampering's wreaking

on existing populations. I'm the right person, I'll tell them,
because I'm drawn to sinkholes and streambeds,

to the gelid and the deeply benthic, because I've a fondness
for cephalic appendages like tiny oars, because I'm smitten

by their licked-y-split high-tailing it out of a pickle, making
like Houdini when confronted with the squish of my rain boots.

Gift Tower

When I read *Siddhartha* in Mrs. Stevens' World Lit class,
the problem I had was reconciling the somber, skinny,

beneath-the-lotus-tree Buddha with the smiling,
fat-bellied, shiny golden Buddha beside the register

at Mei-Ling Shanghai, Metuchen's only *ethnic* restaurant.
It's like when I open the Harry & David Christmas catalogue

with its red-blushed orbs made to look like they spent
the night in the dewy air, when in fact they've been sprayed

with ethylene gas, droplets meticulously arranged
by a food stylist. When I see that sheen on the skin

of a fruit, I think about the skin of the person
who picked it, down there in Medford, Oregon,

glistening with sweat or rain or both, and I don't
have to tell you how much they're getting paid

to pack the Moose Munch Popcorn for the Crater Lake
Gift Basket Classic, which, maybe they're thrilled,

cuz now they can purchase a flat-screen, an Xbox One,
buy now, pay later, thanks to Royal Riviera Pears,

wrapped in golden cellophane, emanating incongruous joy.

Ode to Autocorrect

Because it changes O'Hare to o hate,
o hate, o hate—over and over, no matter
how many times I retype it. O hate, like

an American tune, an American fable
where, yo, you can enter an o hate
bathroom, take a selfie in the mirror

cuz your sister wants to see the pockets
of your Great American Rhinestone Jeans.
Because, on a street called Viewpoint,

I get home becomes *I get guns*, off a road
on a mission to kill every squirrel-ish
pedestrian. Because he was packing,

concealed, threatening to use it, use
his hands or feet. *My feet*, iamb
of a son of a birch, of a brick chatting

with the devil, with God, with a listener
not listening. Because he'd gone bonnets,
his garden bounty a faded wine, his wife's

linguine longing for a golden ear,
so I took her to the botanical gardens
in my getaway car, to a fruit on a vine,

but the limes went lemur, the night to nonfat,
the clear to catastrophic. Because driving away
from the *frog man* croaking hypocrite,

heavenly went down like a melting hedge,
a gal gone hog-tied, a fish crying, a tiger-
tiger togetherness, flight or fucked,

a heart, stroked, racing to its vicarious
carousel, a fungus lashed to a beam gone
beleaguered. Because he will kill her,

that's his plan: to kill us all. Can't commit
or commute, can't debone his breath,
can't take his acute paranoia, chalk it up

to cute. Because this here's a Josie
madhouse, a bedroom bedrock-locked.
Because *Blvd* morphed to *Bled,* spirit

summoned with a Ouija board. Because
soap holder went *love hen,* though love
had flown the Calycanthus

like the grilled portabellos messing
with his vowels. Please *please,* I pleaded
to the pleading day. Because prayer

is like a bread line, a penny for your
exploded mind. Because *lots of logs
to you,* ma, because *so sorry* went *poem.*

Jealous

of that star in Orion
that isn't a star
but a nebula
giving birth to 100s
of infant stars;
if I'm not half
as helpful, a force
against the dark,
then I'm as green
as just-mown Astroturf,
as the monster my daughter
insists is under her bed
with the lime Hi-Chews,
the balls of chartreuse yarn
she never did make
that macramé parrot with.
Jealous like Medea,
who doused her hubby's
flavor-of-the-week with fiery
brew, like the girl who pulls
the braids of the girl she wishes
she could be but can't
because her mother won't buy her
white patent-leather go-go boots,
nor will she be spending spring break
in the Bahamas. *Oh, jealousy*,
Natalie Merchant croons, nodding,
tossing her locks until heck,
she's making us jealous of her
Oh, jealousy. Jealous of the thief
who shoplifts cake mix, shortening,

a couple tubs of pink goop,
so she can bake her kid
a birthday cake, of a thief
because jealousy steals more
than ten white tapers ever will,
though not jealous of the crickets
stuck in a gecko cage, fat & happy
as they crowd an apple core
at the table of thanks, while inside
a fake rock sleeps the un-chirp-able.
Jealous, though, of their easy envy
of the uncaged; they know nothing
of prizes and preaching, of poverty,
though maybe a lot about loss, but not
what it means when the radio says
holed up, at large, fleeing. Loved ones
& armed. Says *scene*, which today
was a place where people eat.
Says *senseless* says *shot says shooter,*
says *shoot shoot shoot,* but aha,
the crickets are silent, are digging
into the soft, sweet flesh of a Honey Crisp,
all for one like Melville described
extracting ambergris from whales,
elbow to unjealous elbow, or so it appears
crickets don't covet another cricket's chirp,
another cricket's cercus or palps.
though who am I to assume? I know
we all have wants, a desire to watch
Orion rise in the eastern dark, find

the fuzzy star that isn't a star
in Orion's sword, home in
on that cloud of dust and gas,
stare for so long I forget
my nephew and I will never agree
about guns, who uses them
and when, forget who I am,
what I don't have, what I didn't
win, stare without resentment
at the cold night, at the place
where a whole bunch
of the future is being born.

Adjacent to the way

she'd been feeling
which had been a kind of

did you turn off the hose?
she was perpendicular

to the hole he'd been digging
to the sequins that fell

from a lavender dress and then
because illusions are always lurking

she saw the lilac bushes listing
and doubt is an empty bucket

because the neighbor's return
from the Arctic equaled giddiness with faith

and though sparking it up equaled a trip
to Yakima the lawn mower seemed a good idea

though handing it over had her thinking
more than normal which was of course

the logical progression though not
in an A-to-B sort of way

more a jagged-y jag like the ants do
when they see him coming at them

with his spit

The Trilobites

All that week I'd wanted to delve
into the late Devonian, when the order
that had held on 270 million years,
began its certain demise. To study

their spiny reign, their hashtag
horizontals, their triple-tined horns.
To do-si-do with their nodes, their spins,
their pits. 20,000 species strong, nearly

every adaptation adventitious to attracting
a mate—periscoping eyestalks, shovels
and scoops fantastically sprung, Liberacian
flourishes and fins—their version of dress

to impress, of petticoats and wigs, of winning
the battle for the sexiest mate. Had wanted
when wanting wasn't enough. *Call Discount Tire.*
If you don't have an author last name, use

a shortened title. Milk, cheese, bread.
Statement of Teaching Philosophy. Forms
for Camp Sealth. When at last bathed,
read, brushed, tucked, kissed, when

put away and wiped, when the house,
except for water surging through pipes,
what I found reminded me of the Romans—
diverse and dispersed, with similar modes

of shucking their mortal coils, in-the-buff coitus
stripped of shame, with whomever, in orgiastic raves
rivaling a Pompeii bath house. Intricately patterned
with curlicues, tubercles, a gill-branched gang

partial to conga-lines crescendo-ing, flashfloods
upstaging the stiffest, dirtiest martini toasts.
One minute flung out and loose, strutting
their scandalous prongs, the next rolling up

in impenetrable balls not unlike our own reaction
to fire and smoke, momentum meltdown, to pumice
and mud letting loose, slides engulfing entire towns,
familiar battening-down against Agnes, Irene, Ike.

In 1969, while digging in the yard, my father cracked open
a sandstone slab, revealed the ones preceding
our stately maples and oaks, our starlings and squirrels,
our 271 Grove. Had wanted to delve, was delving;

had wanted to be swept as they'd been swept,
from *purchase crickets, pay Syd, water seedlings.* They,
who had not seen it coming; I, at any moment,
caught in the same rush.

Screaming Skulls, and the Like

...in the dark there's no quibbling / how readily the world shrugs us off...
—Bob Hicok

and in the slow-as-sediment-building-a-mountain's
gathering light, a pinkish glow, a rippling like I'm supposed

to forget the beetles waiting it out in the duff. I read somewhere
Shelley's death was self-inflicted, but the *Don Juan's*

sail-to-hull ratio was far too high, but the surfeit of pig iron,
far too little freeboard. All his life a passion for boats,

but could the author of "The Triumph of Life" have been unable
to swim? The sun's in my eyes, but still the rusty can

of maggots on Barnegat Bay, beneath the house on stilts,
fish heads left to rot. Do flowers bloom from cadavers?

Of course they do; I saw as much as I lay resting in the grass
dotted with white daisies my daughter and her bestie

chained around their necks. Sitting there where allied bombing
had toppled every medieval stone house, I strained to imagine

swarming flies, the rubble carted away. One accounting
optimistically shared the obliteration afforded

a superior view of the Chateau de Caen. I have to admire
that degree of cup-half-full, like encountering a tray

of taxidermied swifts, their tiny Kleenex-wad eyes,
all the while humming *you got a long, long time*

till you grow old. I wanted the dawn's early light to eradicate
the dead deer on the side of the road as I rounded the last bend

on the Cow Creek Road, just before timber mill stench eclipsed
my middle-of-nowhere lie. Couldn't drive fast enough

past the hunched shoulders of vultures bounding and flapping,
my having disturbed their repast. Which elicits more foreboding:

a roiling steel-gray sea, or a glinting moment of blindness?
I'd venture to say some days it doesn't matter,

a shrugging either/or. I'd venture to say rain or shine,
bring a shovel—the sharpest one you've got.

Beneath twelve feet of ashy topsoil,

pebbles, more ash, lapilli stones, yet more ash,
carbonized wood, hardened volcanic sand,

green-gray pumice, gray pumice, white pumice,
shower of little stones, here they are: the blue-glass

pitcher, snake bracelet, bowl in the shape of a shell.
Here's the bronze speculum, tools for extracting,

for pulling back skin, the bloodletting suction cup.
Here, the scales for weighing, by the libra, by the unicae,

eel and octopus, almonds and broad beans, peaches
and dates; here the ruddy amphorae, two-handled

vessels housing garum, fruit sauce, oil; here, the bread
divided into eighths, stamped with the baker's name:

Celar, slave of Granius Verus. Here, the bronze headrest
broken off from some triclinium's couch, dining room

of the rich, where it was bad luck to sup with less than three
or more than nine (for the Graces, for the Muses), many-

coursed meals, every morsel of mackerel, each lentil and olive,
washed down with ubiquitous wine. Couch on which feasters

reclined. Here, the seventeen silver coins found in the House
of Successus, beside a skeleton. Here they are, or were, detail

of a sandal, woman with child succumbing to Earth's boiling-over
porridge. They had bathed for hours, argued, gossiped, sighed

as they traveled from steam to sauna, to destrictorium, room where oil
and sweat were scraped. Finished up, as for eons, in the frigidarium.

A day beginning like any other—bird song, incessant barking,
scent of baking cakes, a vendor's piercing shouts; a day

whose end no gods or shrines, no jewels or coins, could stop.

The New Nature Poem

will reside in the lattice of latrines,
will sway with horizontal parataxis,

will writhe in plastic, cavort with PCBs,
will sport a durable poly-resin deer

alongside a real mass-wasting deer
browsing on Garry oak seedlings

restoring a smoldering grove. Will have,
instead of a tail in its mouth, the word

sprawl, instead of an ocean, corroding
barrels of nuclear waste crowding its floor,

instead of nostalgic reverence, an unfixed
indigenous drum leaking Agent Orange,

instead of false-construct pastoral,
a Micronesian bomb-test victim's leukemia,

instead of Prelapsarian pastoral bliss,
the poison in the soul of a pineapple.

In the new nature poem, Wranglers and XLTs
loop de loop along the surf, lovers smooch

to the tune of a finless porpoise die-off.
In this poem with its home on the range

of dictions, with its widening swath
of viscous bitumen, with its goopy spill,

its Navajo insult, its Duwamish denial
of federal recognition, with its space for both

the visible and invisible, with its nipping
and tucking of restorative timeless, with its not-

even-quasi religious, the rubbish bin spilling
empties from its craw will not be cordoned off,

and Febreze-ing the outhouse will be outlawed.
All binaries banished, replaced by an embrace

of leaf blower and bunchberry, wrap-around redwood deck
and big-fin bobtail squid, cesspool and untarnished tarn,

belly-up tortoise and Hessel's hairstreak, premiere pre-fab
and custom eco-cabin, Mancala and satellite dish.

If you touch this poem, wear gloves for the Roundup
it romps in, a mask for the endocrine-disrupting pesticides

drifting from its Central Valley in a climate-altering,
drought-induced cloud that spans stanzas, bridges, highways,

penetrates windows and screens, toward your very own
exit ramp, toward your what-you-thought-was-pristine.

This eco-spectacle, rife with bursting-with-asbestos
Glad bags, glutted with groves once grooving,

now gloomy with strip mall and big box, where
Caterpillar 797s, dozers and drillers, where dumping

and fracking, where you just might catch
the trill of a white-crowned sparrow, spot

a California poppy, a heal-all squeezing through a crack,
but mostly where weed whackers whine, where jet skis

mow down spinning phalaropes, mostly airbrushed rivers,
waterfalls torn in half, replaced with a billowing smokestack,

with beak-deformed swallows, albino weasels, wisents
munching moss where radiation levels spike

to Everest heights, down a piece to a phosphate-choked
stream, an un-eco-friendly detergent 0% green. Guaranteed,

beside each saxifrage, each nodding onion, a tailings pond
and a landfill, a stench that'll make you long for a whiff

of smashed skunk. Reaching out to soothe you,
the twisted arms of the last of three species of endemic

sea stars ripping themselves apart, arms crawling away in

Scorching Sinkhole Renga

opposite directions, insides spilling out.
Taking out the trash.
Sickle ablaze in the west,
goddess at her side.

Bought a brand-new toilet,
hauled old one to dump.
Snowdrop glowing white.

Thin and streaky clouds
on a blue-gray backdrop.
America-first sky.

Was-bare birch in my
neighbor's yard. Something
hangs. Catkins or strobiles?

Choosing firmest lemons,
pears least likely to brown:
not the way to shop.

Neon sign in distance,
obscured by rain in sheets:
Climate change a hoax.

Letting the cat in
for Friskies Meaty Bits.
L is for litter, landfill.

Wind stirs up dry leaves.
Let's be so quiet
we can hear the robin's wings.

Spaghetti and Fox.
He put Iran *on notice*?
Same moon. Different world.

Nearly Every Songbird on Earth Is Eating Plastic

nearly every rip is a crisp pact,
nearly every step is a disabled piss,
a slip, a *psst*, is past, is past

the squawking headline, below
the photo of a juvenile herring gull
clasping in its beak, sailing in its scat,

ridding from its ass the remains
of a Yoplait parfait. In 1960, 5%
of sea-faring avians ate plastic.

In 1960, fewer sporks, fewer caps,
fewer cigarette tips. By 1980,
the number had jumped to 80%,

a stirrer, straw, & Starbucks lid
explosion, global production
doubling by the decade, global lips

parting, global rods casting, global
disablers digging, global dips
subtracting. By 2028, more water bottles

swirling in that gargantuan garbage
gyre, that loosely collected rubbish
spectacle, than all the plastic

factory-spat since plastic-ing began.
When auklets stab at shrink wrap,
when pigeon guillemots gulp

Doritos bags, there's no room
in a gut for a mollusk, a morsel
of crab. Punches holes

in their organs. Strips parts. Scraps
scripts. When birds chew Blow Pop
wrappers, guzzle Ziplocs,

courtship desists. When one bird
eats 200 pieces. When one bird's
track departs. Subtract how many

there were, take two away
from three. Take away: a voice
vamoosing, an attic collapsing,

a number deeply dinged, teetering
on cast away, on doused,
on dropping to nil.

Still Life with Motorcycle Revving, Wailing Siren, American Goldfinch Trill

Still life with cell phone, sorrel, beeping alarm.

    Still life with hovering flies, jet heading south toward SeaTac, 6:25.

Still life with crying toddler, catkins, arugula badly needing thinning.

    With gnat swarm, half-empty glass of wine, one struggling ant

floating atop. Still life that will never be a still life, will never be,

    still I imagine what Dali, with his flair for the grandiose,

with his love of everything Velazquez, would make of this most vernal

    of vernal equinox. If I were Dali (*jee jee jee jee jee*) the grass

would morph to a carpet of toothy smiles. As Dali, the kale sprouts

    mustachioed. But no, no, too easy—Dali cannot be reduced

to floating lips, a flourish of facial adornment. Yet, if Dali got his hands

    on this yard, on this psyche, he'd anoint them *Garden Caused*

by the Flight of a Gilded Flicker Around an Andalusian Dog a Second

    Before the Next Siren; Past-due Blossoms with Devotion

and Longing; Poplar of the Inscrutable Conundrum; The Yellow Cedar of Ponderous Faucet. All the while the robin cheery-upping its ass off.

Dali sailing off on a landlocked paddleboard, where Dali, I'm sure, embracing

the local beach scene in a town where the green stuff's legal.

Oh, Dali.

Sometimes you disturb me. When I pilgrimaged to St. Petersburg

for a glimpse of your soupy violins, your lynched eggs,

your hallucinating toreador, *je me sentai pleine*, though a little unnerved.

Always, you were strange like Venus decked out in drawers,

in pom-pom pasties, like a white lobster replacing a telephone's receiver,

initially jarring, though really what better ear-piece to commune

with the populace? A faculty for Lorca-inspired tour de force

is why I bequeath you a yellow-rumped warbler's *chug-a-chugga-chug*

of admiration. Witnessing your waxed mustache tango, I'm a little immortal—

un peu artistique—like I could—when the sirens cease, when the engines,

when the cranky child melts like a goopy blue clock, possess your fluent grace,

a vibrant spurge—alive and lime-y, drunk with persistent excess.

Hummingbirds of the World

God must've been toking some righteously resinous bud
when he dreamed up these iridescent sparklers, these hairy-

tongued sylphs sipping daily from a thousand flowers,
thirteen licks per second. Some kind of altitudinous, uber-crisp

exuberance begot these rubies and mangoes, these hearts lub-
dubbing 250 times a minute, these glitter-bellies eating to live

to the tune of one-hundred times the metabolism of an elephant,
brains 4.2 percent of their total weight, so they may recall not only

every quince, mimosa, weigela, flame acanthus, and trumpet creeper,
but the time it takes each bud to deliquesce. Adam receives

the Outstanding Namer of the Year Award for streamertail,
starthroat and tufted coquette, steely-vented amazilia,

the black-thighed puffleg, the gorgeted sunangel,
the rufous-webbed brilliant. All hail, torpor! Nifty knack

for lowering to thirty degrees the thermostat on a hot-house
baud, in this way surviving April, heartbeat slowed

to a humpback whale's. Bearded mountaineer, empress
brilliant, fire crown, coronet, you are all *joyas voladoras*, for you

I blanket the yard with foxglove, Hot-Lips Salvia, little cigar.

Time for art in the cosmos is very short,

but I brought my colored pencils, sketched
what I saw, the rainbow embracing our world,

fading to fathomless dark. But only for an hour
or so. Then, like a crimson *kokoshnik*, headdress

of old Mother Russia, the sun, once again,
on the rise. That ecru wound like the backbone

of a sauropod? The Grand Canyon. Skull
of a moose? The Great Lakes. Moscow, ember

of a dying fire. Liquid paint would bobble, float
out of reach; oil could damage the instruments.

With my pencils I sketched an azure Africa,
savannahs in flames, the Nile's spider-web

meanderings, its verdant strip of green.
Often I only had time to take notes—

dark blue ... there, washed out. Learned the color
of water depends on its depth, its floor, whether

the sea is choppy or calm. Freed of obstructions,
air and haze, reached a place of pure brightness,

unprecedented clarity. Came to view Earth
as a finite thing, atmosphere thinner

than the thinnest skin. I could stare for hours,
unable to look away, but strict arrangements

forced me back—pencils and sketchbook,
my solitary exuberance, stored for later use.

This highway's a ribbon,

and this is where the ribbon
ends, oily and slick, gray
bridge over gray water.
This is where the ribbon
frays, bumper to bumper
to 7A, Shoulder Closed
and every leaf in flames.
In this asphalt forest,
rubus made for you and me,
laced with butadiene, paradox
and illusion intertwining
like these brambles
with the English Ivy. Yellow
poplars yell at the dog
with its head out the window,
at the lumber-lumbering trucks,
while a sign announces,
with arrows in three directions,
Only, Only, Only. Me-n-my blinker;
you-n-your lane, all of us Legacies
because we're the thread in the fabric
of America's freeway system,
a golden valley dreamed up
by GMC, all of us American
Dream drupes too poisonous
to eat. As I was driving I saw
those endless brake lights,
saw you joining the blood-
orange maples, tailpipes wagging

for the goop extracted, spewed
into lakes, sounds, seas; sulfur
and silicates sloughing from tires
into creeks. All of us messing
with the pH, screwing up
the salmon's gumption to spawn,
while scattered on the median,
impossibly magenta, innumerable
spent-butterfly wings. This land
Tacoma-choked, Rubicon-
riddled, XLT, 370Z.
From the .com castle
to the PCB-laden waters,
this land is made for making
time, good time. For Focus
and Fusion. For Escape.

III. Escape Velocity

Bumblebees Are Made of Ash

The day is a dragonfly hovering in the Timothy. It could rain for months
before the sun goes down. An orange buoy bobs while a sparrow
sings through a wall. The world smells of cedar, skunk spray,
a sedge's sharp edge. The cat's ears clear their throats,
prepare to speak. Kinnell called it "the inexhaustible
freshness of the sea." As if you could imitate
a preening cormorant. As if she'd said *can't*
learn this way, but you heard *can't live*,
destiny's dangling web. A horse
82 miles from its barn while
your brain swings open
like a giant pink
gate.

Space Probe Pantoum

Voyager 1 is leaving home.
Solar winds have slackened.
We didn't know; we didn't know
there'd be a transition zone.

Solar winds have slackened.
Particles from here and there: hello!
Who knew there'd be a transition zone
at the edge of a windless edge.

Particles from here and there: hello!
When the poles switch we'll be certain.
At the edge of a windless edge,
in a zone we've never known.

When the poles switch we'll be certain.
Unexpected, this zipping and zooming
in a zone we've never known.
We call this part the bow shock.

Unexpected, this zipping and zooming.
We're safe here with our sun.
We call this part the bow shock.
The exit, they say, will be rough.

We're safe here with our sun.
Not like a footprint on the moon.
The exit will be rough,
won't be all at once,

not like a footprint on the moon.
Like some strange angel,
it won't be all at once.
Flitting around on the fringe

like some strange angel,
we know we're nearly there,
flitting around on the fringe.
Us stuff nearly gone,

we know we're nearly there.
Voyager I is leaving home,
us stuff nearly gone:
we didn't know; we didn't know.

Because the Dead Never Vanish

Sand in your shoes
Take them off at the door!
Another silent argument
(a bottle in the bilge) Ferried
her reclusive river—vanished
in a bellyful of wine

In a river named Myakka
In a county known for its sand
In a state known for its vanished
In a country where the ferry
points toward Lethe—its bilge
like a belly (no arguing allowed)

Her belly never filled never full
Cruel river with mangroves
Down on your cypress knees picking
an argument down on your sandy
knees before the details vanish
while the ferryman loads his passengers

because a ferry is never full
because a belly is never fooled
because the dead never vanish
because a river is a meandering reminder
because the sand is remainder
because no one can argue otherwise

I don't want that argument she said
I don't want to board that ferry
falling from her mouth like sand
Craving only a belly knows
Mot juste only a river knows
(vanished at the mouth)

vanished like fish bones like mist
like an argument you can't win
like a river's unreachable headwaters
while the ferry turns in the other direction
like a sandy shoe from its mate
like wine in the belly of a whale

Ode to a Red Bell Pepper

As if you'd walked straight into this room
from a sweltering field, not stopping to wipe

the sweat from your muscled, aching back.
Burnished, burning misery of lugging laden

crates in 110-degree heat. Fruit suited up
for gym class in scarlet bloomers concealing

a spray of seeds like ray-less tansy.
Buxom capsicum, you're blushing;

your amplitude's noted as you belt out
Red, Red Wine as if this table's a karaoke

dive bar, all-night $2 wells. *You feel so fine,*
you partial bust of Venus, Archaic Torso

of Scarlet, you with your cheery thighs
like Picasso's acrobats, that briefest period.

You, the weepy drip no mother of mine
would speak of. Glint in the baby-making

suite. You: curvaceous darling suggesting
a womb, fear's pulsing bulb. An emergency.

Vermilion bird on a night with no moon.

Life on Mars

After traveling 93,000,000 miles on a ship called Orion,
we arrive. Each of us has grown two inches,
spines extending into darkness.

Our bones are brittle, our livers press into our hearts.
We're less nimble, but we carry, in our pressurized
suits, The Spirit of Humanity.

We're thirsty like seeds, like seedlings, like the animals
we are, but we must plow to find ice, melt it, distill it.
Speaking of blue,

there will be none. Speaking of alone, to make air
hydrogen and oxygen must be split apart,
mixed with argon. Once we have it,

we'll breathe. We will terraform, re-engineer the atmosphere,
make it Palm Springs. Streambeds will flow
like the Skagit at flood stage.

It must be home because there are zero-gravity luxury hotels,
virtual reality experience on the holodeck, live streaming
with loved ones via high-speed wireless.

Off-Earth children will gather for bedtime stories about the fiery skipper
and the mourning cloak, a planet where sunsets were painted
with a many-colored broom.

The Mechanical Hope Contraption

It did not swoop on me, the barred owl,
but perched on a streetlamp, illumed

where cedars sipped the first few drops
of autumn rain. It did not swoop, nor

could I sense its resilience; I was slow
like the long way around the lake, like oars

in a muddy slick, yet to witness the crepuscular
felt like grace, raccoons skulking the upper trail.

I couldn't taste tenacity, what drives a creature
to wipe the dirt from its face, remount

the mechanical hope contraption, not
an actual horse but a scrap-metal bronco

forged by an off-the-grid hillbilly in darkest
Arkansas. Nuzzling belief, an honest-to-God

mane, I'd watched my uncle grip the reins
of the stand-in, endure a rope-induced kilter,

thrown and humbled both. He had fallen
but the morning didn't end, just kept going,

barn after barn, anonymous horse after horse.
I do not like the word *redemption*, would rather

not refer to these dawn-roaming creatures
as holy survivors of the Anthropocene. I'll take

the memory of a man who could name every
mushroom from Pennsylvania to the Gulf.

Oh, Jerry

A horizon like aluminum foil smeared with pink lip gloss.
Crows flying from their roosting spots to their daytime haunts.
BVDs and Dickeys whipping in the wind.

Jerry here. Our records show your Legacy is due for an oil change.

Oh, Jerry. So much radiator fluid.

I got knocked up she's a teenager.

Also, Jerry, remember the time I took a left out of your shop and a wheel slid off its axle?

She came out gray, coated in vernix. Cord around her neck.

When your text came in, she was asking if I'd seen the link about minimalism? *If it doesn't bring you joy, if you wouldn't buy it if you saw it in a store.*

When your text came in, I was wondering if her nausea might be cramps.

Jerry?

We sold the Legacy; it kept breaking down. We bought an Outback, drove it seven hours south and off the grid.

Tornado

Seven driveways bereft of their houses,
their two-car garages. Bottle of body mist

balanced on a bureau; on a chest of drawers,
a cable box, while two hours away in Broken

Arrow, a cancelled check flutters to the ground.
Like the school was flying, someone said, someone

lodged in the eye, in a place where the drill
was *tuck up, wait it out,* where Jennifer Doan,

newly pregnant, wrapped a dozen students
in her arms as the walls let go. With fractured

sternum and spine, with a length of rebar
jutting into her side, listened to the ones

below her: *I can't hold this rock much longer,*
then no sound at all. *You could taste the dirt*

falling from the ceiling, smell the gas, hear
the pounding at the door shut tight as we could,

this once-in-a-million happening twice
in fourteen years, June Simson crying

on the shoulder of Jo McGee beside a row
of concrete slabs, seven driveways leading to nowhere.

Lately my gratitude's

out of bounds like the soccer ball the blue team kicked into suspecting arms.

Not quite drifting off, more like a shit-storm of sex acts, the shenanigans of giants

live-streaming through my cranium's Prime, a podcast of characters I don't recall

serving me ice cream, roping a tree to the top of my car. What I'm saying is my transition

from awake to not is when the pilot says bumpy air, pings the seatbelt sign. My battery

doesn't cycle quietly. I'm tired but my mind's tracking down the bearded lady and the frog

man. This is when I start what must be praying, litany of what and who, which is

everything from fingerless gloves to the gal on 50th and Genesee who hems my jeans. I

give thanks to buckwheat tea and in-home heating. Also, to the smell of my daughter's part

when I kiss it goodnight, like an animal fresh out of hibernation. By the time my

Greyhound Bus kicks into snore I'm thanking the stillness, that our bed's not shaking, that

the missile imploded on its launch pad, that the war between fake and real went armistice.

Insaning off to sleep like making sense of the *Book of Revelation,* battle between the beasts of

the earth and sea versus biting into the flesh of a Tennessee Walker. My brother says it

boils down to the Anti-Christ, prophesized temple in the Fertile Crescent. Lake of fiery

brimstone, my cranium's spewing neuron volcanoes of appreciation. Hi-jinx like what goes

on in a waste treatment plant, never sure what will surface—false teeth, a shuttlecock, a set

of keys, a basin of serpents, of which I thank each one.

Yes, of course

those are angels lighting up
the neon, the eroding E
on your laptop keyboard. Not
a ghost, not a sign, but one

of God's bonafide lackeys.
What if the prominence
and the coronal hole told each other
they were beautiful? What if this

was the beginning of an eclipse?
Misery might have wings,
but it also has a mane, antlers,
a muzzle. Sometimes a shell

holds a current of melting doubt,
a slurry of cinnamon-colored truth.
Praying can happen at any time,
peeling back the leathery skin,

slicing into a mango. The years
marry all the sunsets since
the very first—every green flash,
whether or not they exist.

Peach Glosa

Ah! And red; and they have peach fuzz, ah!
They are full of juice and the skin is soft.
They are full of the color of my village And
of fair weather, summer dew, peace.

Slid out of me like stones,
like peonies and roses,
pricked like a holly bush,
lulled me with the hymns of weevils.
Loud like the lion that can kill,
flew out of me like cheetahs,
took hold of me like lice, like love.
Ripped me open like a cougar.
Rose up at me like a cream-bellied cobra.
Ah! and red; and they have peach fuzz, ah!

Clattering and weeping. Diapering
and digging. Exuberant singing,
firecats leaping. Peaches, more
peaches! Crates of velvety freestones.
In a basket, at breakfast, with a wasp.
Hail, pale stranger, come down
from the Kunlun Shan Mountains.
Beware of leaf curl, brown rot, beware
the speckled emperor, the catapult moth.
They are full of juice and the skin is soft.

Bloodmeal, bonemeal, stunted growth.
Peach wood arrows to shoot away evil; peach
wood wands to ward away the bad.
Caravaggio's memorable discolorations,

molted and wormholed, Monet and Rubens
speaking the truth, through peach and leafage,
from their hearts and tongues. Budded or grafted
from a suitable rootstock. Budded or grafted,
my dear luscious darlings, my dappled courage.
They are full of the color of my village.

They grow like stars. They grow like mountains,
like fissures, an inch or six a year. Measure
themselves against a lazy yellow wall. Compete
to see who'll ripen first. Stevens said,
of parenting, it's a "terrible blow to poor
literature," Holly, peach of his reason,

pen stilled till she reached the age of nine,
firecat closing his big, bright eyes.
They are not ours, not ours to keep, spice
of fair weather, summer dew, peace.

I am the miraculous

the traffic running smoothly down Oak, the octopus's
three-tenths-of-a-second transformation from algae-leaf sprig

to many-tentacled astonishment. I'm the sacs and cells
that brought you into focus, the aqueous humour, the hyaloid canal

that gave you sight. I am every bit of physics–escape velocity,
magnetism (weak and strong), the mechanics of fluids,

the vectors and the vitreous, the noble gases, the birthing
and dying of stars. I am lightning's formation, pipes and pumps,

pressure and power, the heat that is lost, the voltage rising.
I'm your blood's pH, the trillions of microbes spinning

and twirling on every inch of your skin, the loud-and-clear-
from-two-miles-away whistling gibbon, the screaming vixen,

howl of the socially satisfied wolf. All of me summed up
in one small artifact: a pair of fornicating froghoppers

entombed in sap. My sister: the helicopter dropping
5,000 tons of sand and clay and lead. My brothers:

the quarter million enlisted who climbed to life-
time exposure, received *a unique clean-up medal.*

My children: I bore thousands, each one named *Incredulous.*
Their children, the owls who fly to their breeding grounds

at the coldest hour of night.

Break-Away Effect

In a study published in the April 1957 issue of Aviation Medicine, 35 percent of training astronauts and cosmonauts reported having experienced a strange feeling of having broken the bonds of the terrestrial sphere. Psychologists referred to this phenomenon as the break-away effect.
    —Mary Roach, *Packing for Mars*

As if my body were a door or gate, cabinet
bereft of its rational rations, they worried

I'd unhinge, become the lunatic saboteur.
They barred my hands from touching

their switches and dials, my access
to the manual. And here I am—

surprise!—your peaceful giant,
benevolent king of the cosmos;

it's all I can do to keep from belting out
The Motherland hears, the Motherland knows /

where her son flies in the sky. Down there,
every sunset's a smashed egg; up here,

dusk's a pink-cheeked *devochka*, a violet
violence, orange of longing stilled. They said

I'd panic, shock of fathomless vacuum akin
to slicing a kayak through the Bering Strait,

never having commandeered a pair of paddles
freed from their clips. Instead, I'm glued

to the porthole, to the wispy beards of mountains,
stray-hair rivers, lemony fields of wheat, light

as if streaming from the stained glass of Pokrovsky
Cathedral. Each dawn a powder-blue halo,

and me with just one wish: to never return.

Also by Martha Silano:

What the Truth Tastes Like
Blue Positive

The Little Office of the Immaculate Conception
The Daily Poet (as co-author)
Reckless Lovely

Gravity Assist was printed using the font Adobe Garamond Pro.

www.saturnaliabooks.org